D0423185

by
the
light
of
the
silvery
mc
lune
:
media
parables
poems
signs
gestures
and
other
assaults
on
the
interface

BY THE LIGHT
OF THE SILVERY McLUNE:
MEDIA PARABLES
POEMS
SIGNS
GESTURES
AND OTHER ASSAULTS
ON THE INTERFACE

LIONEL KEARNS

THE DAYLIGHT PRESS

Copyright © 1969 by Lionel Kearns

OTHER BOOKS BY LIONEL KEARNS

Songs of Circumstance, Tish Press, Vancouver, 1963.
Listen George, Imago Press, Montreal, 1965.
Pointing, Ryerson Press, Toronto, 1967.

This book is published jointly by the DAYLIGHT PRESS,
3358 W. First Ave., and TALON BOOKS.

VANCOUVER, B.C., CANADA

dedicated to George Bowering

\

"RISE UP AND ABANDON THE CREEPING MEATBALL!"
Y.I.P.

ACKNOWLEDGEMENTS: These poems have appeared in various forms and under various titles in the following magazines: *Ambit, Ant's Forefoot, Blue Ointment, Canadian Forum, Delta (Canada), Edge, El Corno Emplumado, Georgia Straight, Imago, Open Letter, Outposts, Prism International, Quarry, Tish, Tlaloc, Volume 63, West Coast Review, Work;* anthologies: *The Golden Convulvus,* Blackburn, 1965. *Commonwealth Poems of Today,* London, 1967. *Vietnam Committee Broadside,* Vancouver, 1967. *The New Romans,* Edmonton, 1968; and radio: The Canadian Broadcasting Corporation, "Anthology"; recordings: *See-Hear.*

Our gratitude is also extended to the Canada Council, whose financial support aided the author in completing this work and the publishers in its publication.

TABLE OF CONTENTS

Note: THE BIRTH OF GOD is a mathematical mandala embodying the perfect creative/destructive principle of the mutual interpenetration and balanced interdependence of opposites: one and zero, something and nothing, substance and void, being and oblivion, positive and negative, good and bad, spirit and flesh, black and white, yin and yang, male and female, thesis and antithesis, this and that — and all the possible dynamic relationships of these polarities, the simultaneous representations of which are immediately obvious in the icons of sex, childbirth, and death.

THE BIRTH OF GOD

```
          11111111111
       111111111111111111
     1111111111111111111111
    111111111111111111111111
   11111111111         1111111
   111111111    000    1111111
   1111111    00000    1111111
   11111     0000000   1111111
   11111  000000000    1111111
   11111  000000000    1111111
   11111    0000000    1111111
   1111111  0000000    1111111
   1111111  0000000    1111111
   1111111  0000000    1111111
   1111111  0000000    1111111
   1111111  0000000    1111111
   1111111  0000000    1111111
   1111111  0000000    1111111
   1111111  0000000    1111111
   1111111  0000000    1111111
   1111111  0000000    1111111
   1111111  0000000    1111111
   11111    0000000       11111
   11111 00000000000   11111
   11111 00000000000   11111
   11111 00000000000   11111
   11111               11111
    111111111111111111111
     11111111111111111111
      1111111111111111111
        11111111111
```

ENVIRONMENT

Bent old men and women and dirty children scavenging for
   scraps of paper to pack in immense bundles on their backs
   for a few centavos
They keep the streets clean
They are also shining your shoes and polishing your sports car
   and scrubbing out your toilet bowl
They are puking in their piles of rags
They are pawing through your garbage can for something to
   eat
They are so hungry they will do anything for a drink
They are selling their sick sisters to tourists
They are even pretending to smile
And you are so used to seeing all this that you hardly consider
   it anymore
Or maybe it's because their skins are darker than yours that
   you dismiss it as part of the natural order
But listen to me Fatty
They are living and dying and waiting the slow wait of the
   desperate
Degradation would finish them off if it wasn't for their hatred
And there is a rumour that something is going to happen
The police have begun searching for guns stored in the barrios
(It has happened before in other places, you know)
And don't go putting me down as just another one of those
   social-protest boys
Because I'm not protesting in the least
I'm just telling you what's going on
So you won't be too surprised when it happens

BLEEDING POEM

Bleeding in Patzcuaro
      with freezing moon and bitter *pulque*

    Bleeding on streets
        in *cantinas*
        into my bowl of market-place *mole*

Bleeding in the launch on black Lake Patzcuaro

      Bleeding to Janitzio Island
    with Morelos Colossus
and candied masks of Father Death
        and sputtering candles
    melting on tops of elaborate tombs

    Bleeding amongst the ragged Tarascans
kneeling there in their old *serapes* and straw hats
      and there will be another basket-ball game
Immediately after the Dance of the Moros

      Three Indians in stupid-face
with traditional butterfly fish-nets
        hopping about

There is no music
    MC on malfunctioning PA
      is trying to imitate Augustine Lara:
        Rosa/ La mas hermosa . . .*etc.* . . . .

Everybody Laughs
except old Morelos, revolutionary *bandido*, and now
    awesome witness of lake and island
standing stoney-cold and high into the blackness
        his immense feet
    almost the size of the basket-ball court

        Unseen in the background
this figure present and silently brooding on death himself
    the sacrificial death of violent uprisings
and more the eternal Indian death
        of generations of fathers and children

    Here the communicants
and me bleeding among crowds of watchers and waiters
    shivering under the clank of chapel Mass-bell
        trying to recall
        the black-snatched *putas* of Morelia
who wouldn't participate past their duty

    Thinking more the lying travel-ads
    the misleading local propaganda
and how we are presently standing here
    in the deathly cold of the Day of the Dead
at night, with no boats
        running back to the mainland for our price

But wait till the Indians bring out their grave-juice
(though you have to know the secret words in Tarascan)
   everybody laughs, the priest
     is Augustine Lara: *Rosa*. . .clank clank. . .

   But shouldn't we climb the hill
     and read the graffiti
    scratched on the end of Morelos' big toe?
no, someone will take our place if we move

   Two queer Mexican medical students
   in spotless white pants and tennis shoes
   have bundles of blankets and little
   medicine bottles of Canadian whiskey
   and the one who likes to talk English
   knows Bill's friend the scientist in Montreal
   who tortures rats in stress experiments
   he wants to get chummy under the blanket
   I threaten him with blood and he
   produces a clean white handkerchief

Bleeding bleeding bleeding
     how long will we have to wait?
    when will the dead arrive
    when will we eat?

Liquorice bats and sugar frosted skeletons
whole edible altars with icing lace and taffy chalice
a tin for the tourist coin

The paralyzed girl on the litter makes no noise
the other children are trying to cry
no one puts in any money

Bleeding family members
are waiting for their dead fathers. Everybody laughs
there are also many smaller coffins
some are the size of infants and babes
some are made of candy

There are too many tourists
there is not enough money
Senor, there is not enough money, my wife is sick
see how many of my little ones
are gone already

But we will have them back tonight
that is why everyone is happy
it is the night of the Day of the Dead
it is too cold for guitars
the fishing is very poor

O drink the bitter *pulque* with the orange caterpillar

Eat the bleeding caterpillar in the freezing *mezcal*

O ghostly blood of the bottled worm

The devil worm in the Blakian night of old cold Mexico

Where they are making it into a movie

        It's a kind of travelogue
             and I am bleeding with cold
but why are three of them in top hats
      and that other thin-nosed bastard in a kilt?
    nobody looks at him

        Praying Tarascans and fantastic tombs
sometimes they light fresh candles
      on candied shrines of skull and crucifix
the camera crew stepping on them
      the director shouting
          moving them out of the way

                Floodlights freeze the kneeling children
GET OUT OF THE WAY
                    some cannot understand Spanish
it is very cold and bleeding
                    nobody laughs but the cast
                        because it's in the script

They must shoot that sequence over again
                        walking down from behind the rock
        making their way between flickering candles
                            and entranced families

    the girl in the bikini shivers
under her fur coat. I am bleeding. Augustine Lara
            has been frozen into a pillar of salt
the dead are arriving now

Everybody is eating
            death dolls and candied corpses. Oh stop
oh frozen blood on Janitzio stone
    the secret grave juice, the sacred mushroom
                the ravaging spirits
        of dead fathers and lost brothers
the drying fish-nets
            the wrinkled Tarascan faces
This is the night the dead are with us
                this is the feast of All Souls
        and I alone have nothing to eat

This is the night the sweet-tooth phantoms
                    arrive in town for late dinner
Here is a meal
        prepared on bleak Janitzio Island
            by dying Indians and bleeding watchers

Here you can relish a candied death
                    and Tarascan basket-ball

Here they are making it into a film

See the happy motor-launch owners of Patzcuaro

See the serapes stiff in the frozen dawn

The earth drinks up the death-chill blood

See how it drops and clots in the water

I have left my mark on the boat

The following afternoon we returned to the Capital. The
mountain slopes were covered with flowering yellow bushes
and the sun was so hot that we stopped to bathe in a waterfall
by the side of the road. At dusk we came in sight of the city,
the lights spread out below us twinkling for miles across the
valley. When we arrived there was still time to get a shot of
Vitamin K to stop the bleeding.

17

EXPRESSION

Smashing the wall with your fist
is something to be tranquilly recollected
or talked about years afterwards
drinking with your friends, laughing
smashing the wall with your fist
is absurd and anyway expensive
whether you have to pay the landlord
for the hole in the plaster
or if it was concrete, then
even when you have medical insurance
there's the ex-ray fee and the physio-therapy
smashing the wall with your fist
is a crazy thing to do
but effective too, a way
to instantly change a situation
converting one kind of pain to another
pain you can cope with by groaning
and first-aid, the doctor may give you
a little something, someone is
trying to clean up the mess
smashing the wall with your fist
is better than smashing somebody's face
is perhaps even better
than writing a poem about
smashing the wall with your fist.

WORD

I use it in pointing to
my own madness and desire
to possess you utterly
sometimes perhaps even
to drive your mind from your body

But for you
it is something else
another kind of feeling
love, we
know there is a difference
and I fall asleep troubled
With my arms around you like chains

In the morning
you have my breakfast ready
before I open my eyes

MEDIUM

Your innocence, my fatigue
poetry, the rain
proscribed subjects
objects too trivial
to waste a breath

Once I'd be filling up poems
with outrageous images
    and impossible ideas
just to keep track of them
and let you know I'm here

Now I give you only
silence and blank paper
but this too
    is a kind of message

the woman who
him of the woman who reminded
of the woman who reminded him
the woman who reminded him of
woman who reminded him of the
who reminded him of the woman
reminded him of the woman who
him of the woman who reminded
of the woman who reminded him
the woman who reminded him of
woman who reminded him of the
who reminded him of the woman
reminded him of the woman who
him of the woman who reminded
of the woman who reminded him
the woman who reminded him of
woman who reminded him of the
who reminded him of the woman
reminded him of the woman who
him of the woman who reminded
of the woman who reminded him
the woman who reminded him of
woman who reminded him of the
who reminded him of the woman
reminded him of the woman who
him of the woman who reminded
of the woman who reminded him
the woman who reminded him of
woman who reminded him of the
who reminded him of the woman
reminded him of the woman who
him of the woman who reminded
of the woman who reminded him
the woman who reminded him of
woman who reminded him of the
who reminded him of the woman
reminded him of the woman who
him of the woman who reminded
of the woman who reminded him
the woman who reminded him of
woman who reminded him of the
who reminded him of the woman
reminded him of the woman who
him of the woman who reminded
of the woman who reminded him
the woman who reminded him of
woman who reminded him of the
who reminded him of the woman
reminded him of the woman who
him of the woman who reminded
of the woman who reminded him
the wom...

REMINDED
HIM
OF
THE
WOMAN
WHO
REMINDED
HIM
OF
THE
WOMAN
WHO
REMINDED
HIM
OF
THE
WOMAN
WHO
REMINDED
HIM
OF
THE
WOMAN
WHO
REMINDED
HIM
OF
THE
WOMAN
WHO
REMINDED
HIM
OF
THE
WOMAN
WHO
REMINDED
HIM
OF
THE
WOMAN
WHO
REMINDED
HIM

PERSONALITY

Saint-Denys Garneau used to split up
and actually walk down the street
beside himself, partners so to speak
though one would hardly say chums
But with me there isn't even
               that consolation
You see, it was years ago, and I'd
just staggered off the train after
working three days with no sleep
and as usual I'd drifted all the way
down to Carrall and Hastings
               from the C.P.R. station
Well anyway I said to myself listen
you wait right here
and I'll be back in a few minutes
Then I walked off and never returned
I don't know how long he waited there
I deliberately put him out of my mind
and gradually lost track of him
               completely. Of course
I've been back a few times recently
but there isn't any sign of him now
and even if he'd stayed in that part
of town, do you suppose I could
recognize him now? Do you think
he's still up to the same old tricks
or is he a *new man*?
I wonder if he ever thinks about me?

CONTENT

Each human body a temple of the Holy Ghost said the old nun
And so I developed a passion for religious architecture
Strange but that's the kind of poem I write
Because that's the way I am, though sometimes I remember seeing
A child peeping over the counter of the newspaper kiosk outside the AUTOBUS DE ORIENTE terminal
Cute little Mexicana with black Indian hair and big brown eyes
Until she runs out from behind and before her mother can chase her back
Everyone sees she's got no nose, just a gaping hole where it ought to be
And that's the kind of poem that keeps sneaking up all the time now
Not so much of a *howcome* poem anymore
But moving towards a *well-what-are-you-going-to-do-about-it* kind of poem
And impossible to publish

FOREIGN AID

Relaxing all day in this tropical atmosphere
glass in hand, a mosquito net and fans at night
sweating a bit but never exerting yourself
you think how easy it would be to make it permanent

to become the modern counterpart of the old white planter.
You've met a few of them, no pith helmets now but
they still observe the decencies, dressing for dinner
playing bridge down at the Yacht Club, having cock-tails

with our new High Commissioner. Perhaps you could manage it
as an oil–field specialist or missile tracking technician
British or American, even a Canadian might fit in
as bank manager or some kind of Foreign Aid expert

living on a small portion of your Canadian salary
with four servants and two cars and a house high on the hill
with a sea breeze and white neighbours. What if the wife
flies to New York every few months and the cost

of educating the children is ridiculous, at least
you're still enjoying good liquor and imported food
and in moments of privacy you relish the view
of the young servant on her knees scrubbing the floor

a wonderful creature really, strong, pretty and always cheerful.
Yes they've asked you to be god-father to her second child
and you're so delighted you raise her wages to $40 a month
Oh it's good to be good and still live the good life

and though your face grows redder and redder each year
(because after all a man would be mad to leave all this)
and though your body gets flabbier and you lose your hair
and your paunch sticks out above your khaki shorts, at least

the skin under your clothes seems to be turning even whiter
and you joke about this when you have guests visiting from home
and you're pointing out the interesting features of the local scene
the quaint behavior, for example, of the native population

their inate laziness and lack of initiative, but they're
a happy lot generally. And finally, after years and years
of this pleasant life (and you're still an amiable chap yourself)
quite suddenly, as you are sleeping comfortably

(because of course your bedroom has air conditioning)
you open your eyes in total amazement
in time to meet death in the blackness
on the chopping blades of numberless machetes

METAPHOR

Their meeting
was as strange
as apple blossoms
falling on
a pool of blood

And when at last
they made love
it seemed as though
God himself
was exercising
his imagination

POINTS OF VIEW

Faces of commuters
on the train
        — expressionless
with drudgery
complacent in routine
and me overwhelmed
by the sadness of it
thinking them all
lost, damned
for choosing
        that kind of life

Considering it again
later I realize that
perhaps it's not them
but us
        who are damned
for choosing
        to be human

COMMUNICATION

I'm shy let's
make love then
talk he said

make love then   he said   let's
talk   shy
I'm

talk   he   said
make love then
I'm   shy   let's

make love then
I'm   shy   let's
talk   he   said

make love then
talk   he   said
I'm   shy   let's

talk   he   said
I'm   shy   let's
make love then

I'm   shy   let's
make love then
talk   he   said

THE ANSWER

You will know the answer
when you see it, falling
out of the sky
           on a windy day
splashing in a puddle or
perhaps sitting there quietly
on the table
           staring at you from
between the mango-chutney
           and the soya sauce
For the answer will turn up
in spite of the difficulties
and confusion of dead cats
rotting roses and discarded
           automobile parts
perhaps one day slipping
unobtrusively into the room
to whisper to you in a voice
almost inaudible, or it may
stop you on the street
and instead of asking
           for a match it
will mention the fact casually
as though merely making
           polite conversation
Yes you will recognize
the answer when you meet it
and it will tell you that
           everything is both
possible and impossible
           at the same moment

SCULPTURE

Two fingers in her mouth
two fingers in her snatch
an offering, the epiphany
of a wizened grandmother
timeless and real, a gesture
open and full of meaning.

Two fingers pulling down
                    her lower lip
two fingers stretching
            the beaten labia
the old woman who took shape
from the trunk of a tree
as the carver caressed it
blessed it with his ax

Two fingers tearing her lips
two fingers ripping at her cunt
this figure brought forth
revealed and revealing
Dzu-Nu-Gwa the lady giant
today only three feet tall

THE BUSINESS

She wanted it all but
was too busy
having it
to get on
with the business
of getting it

He too wanted it all but
was too busy
getting on
with the business
of getting it
to have it

TELEPHONE

After completing his call
    Roderick discovered
   the phone-booth had no door
He was sure the door had been there
    when he entered
but there was no mistaking the fact
    that there was no door now

 "Strange"
    he thought to himself
as he examined the ceiling and floor
   for a secret panel
    or emergency exit-hatch
but after going over
   the whole compartment
  with infinite care and attention
he resigned himself to the idea
    that he would be there
   for a long time
     if not indefinitely

32

In the heat of his first panic
         Roderick phoned all his friends
                  telling them
               what had happened
           and asking for advice
                  They all thought
                     it was the funniest story
            they'd ever heard
                  over a telephone
and they said "Yeah Roderick
               that's a good one hohoho
     HOHOHO we'll be right down
           with a wrecking team
                  to get you out"
and one of them even suggested
                  that Roderick listen
           to his new record
                  "It'll blow your mind
     right out of that cubicle"
                  he said
                  but it didn't work
and they never came down
           and soon Roderick
                     had used up
     all the change in his pocket
and after that
           he could only make
                  long-distance calls
     and reverse the charges
but because his long-distance friends
                     were too far away
         they couldn't help him either

33

and soon they began to catch on
to what he was up to
so they stopped accepting
the charges
having realized that Roderick
never sent them any money
to cover the bills

Of course Roderick
tried to communicate directly
with people
on the outside
but these efforts
as one might expect
proved utterly futile
He would tap on the glass
with his bare knuckles
but passers-by would either
pretend to ignore him or just
hurry on their way
going to the office weekdays
or perhaps church
Sunday mornings
though some of them
became so accustomed to seeing
Roderick in the same place
day after day
that they grew somewhat familiar
and would even nod a quick hello
if there was time
or smile and wave good-morning

Roderick
in his desperation
found the one person
he could actually talk to
was the directory girl
who answered when he dialed *Information*
the only number
that could be reached
without first inserting a coin
and he would talk to her
whenever he could
him making up names
with problematical addresses
and then attempting
to talk about the weather
or otherwise pleasantly
pass the time of day
while she searched her lists
and apologized
for taking so much time
and gradually over the years
their relationship developed
and he would repeat
the same old cliché that she
was all the world to him
which in Roderick's case
was the truth

However
from time to time Roderick
found this *information* girl
something less than perfect
for she tended to be jealous
and would accuse him
of chatting up the regular operators
or of having secret dealings
with the boys
in the service department
all of which was quite impossible
for the service department
never answers its calls
and the regular girls
are allowed to say only
"Number please"
"I beg your pardon"
"Thankyou" and
"Please hold the line"
this last phrase being
particularly abhorrent to Roderick
but nevertheless she would accuse him
of this kind of indiscretion
and he would get excited and scream
"You stupid bitch you don't
understand! You don't understand!"
and she would start to cry
and say "Roderick"
I've told you before
if you use that kind of language
I'll never speak to you again"

And she didn't
and this left Roderick
        counting his heartbeats
           hearing himself
        murmur and breathe
    with no one to talk to him
no one to lend an ear in response

And as Roderick's phone-booth
           gradually filled up
      with beard and excrement
shrubs and ivy
  grew up and obscured it
        from the outside
    so that today
no one knows whether Roderick
      is living or dead

INSTRUCTIONS

You hear the words click into place
As you slip them deliberately into the magazine
Then lifting the poem to your shoulder and closing one eye
You squint along the barrel to get things lined up
The dot at the end covering the target, and just visible through
    the V at the back
Calmness and precision. *Squeeze* the trigger, dont't pull it
And if he kicks his legs out stiff and falls flat
You know your aim is true
(So what if the metaphor's too bloody cute? Goddamn it you
    know what I mean!)
Anyway, you must have seen them do it in the movies

A COLLAGE EDUCATION

You saw it too
the TV documentary
on the problem
of Negro ghettos
in American cities
that was chopped up
by spot commercials
for *Vanquish*
the pill that
takes away your
headache
for ever

COMMUNITY DEVELOPMENT

The prisoners have every convenience
Light-weight aluminum-alloy chains
Foam-rubber linings for their manacles, even
The temperature of their cells thermostatically
Controlled. They have good nutricious food
And special hours for recreation. In fact it's
Unknown for them to complain at all, and if you
Ask them they will tell you with the utmost
Sincerity, that life here is good, except
For the occasional disturbance, but they
Can handle that too, like the time that man
Herman the troublemaker started acting up
Asking all sorts of questions and shouting
Those despicable slogans. But the prisoners
Fixed Herman alright, with the co-operation
Of the authorities, and he died there
Stapled to the lavatory wall, a figure
As ignominious as he was absurd, with his
Crazy "Declaration of Love and Liberation"
Twisted around his neck like a collar

DOMESTICITY

She says Reginald are you listening to me
Reginald the man from the finance company
was around again Reginald he says they're
going to take away the T.V. and Reginald
there's the dentist Reginald and the kids
need clothes Reginald and remember you said
we could take a vacation this year Reginald you
promised Reginald you promised and all we get
is more bills Reginald and the car won't even
pass the safety inspection Reginald and
Reginald you said we were going to get
a new car Reginald before we have any
more kids and here I am Reginald
seven months gone already Reginald and
Reginald there's just no hope left anymore
so Reginald you know what we're going to do
Reginald it's the only thing there is now
Reginald it will solve everything Reginald
Reginald you'll have to sell your soul

UNIVERSITY

"Personally," said the Professor
"I'm not altogether opposed
 to security checks on campus
 In fact," he went on
 "with my office bugged
 I feel at last that I'm
 participating directly
 in the Electric Age. Besides
 without RCMP agents, CIA spies
 and those informants
          for the administration
 I wouldn't have anyone at all
 showing up at my lectures"

ABLUTION

Henry would cruise by lighted laundromats
peering in the big front windows
      looking for solitary chicks:
runaway school girls
           hiding out in the city
good-natured widows
      with their hair in curlers
perhaps a lonely wife
             her hubby and kids
      sleeping peacefully at home

    And when he'd spot one
he'd whip in quick
        with his laundry bundle
and he'd be saying "Gosh
   I've forgotten the bleach" or
        "What's the matter
   with this here change machine?"

And pretty soon they'd be
      talking together and smiling
and he'd be singing songs
      and telling jokes
(a rare thing — laughter
      in a midnight laundromat)

And by the time they'd stuffed
                    both their loads
              in the same dryer
                    to save money
and were sitting back
                    watching the yellowy sheets
          and odd socks and holey underwear
                    tumbling tumbling
and were blowing smoke in one another's face
they'd be relating their own life stories
and Henry would end up by suggesting
          "Well dammit why don't I give you
                    a lift home?"

     But Henry had a serious problem
in maintaining a supply of dirty clothes
          so he'd have to tear around
                    during the day
begging bundles off his friends

By now the whole thing
          had become a kind of passionate ritual
                    with Henry having to travel with
          a spare bundle stashed away in the trunk
in case one of his sallies miscarried

Though it was safe to say
                    that Henry
the master romancer of the laundromat night
          seldom failed in a first attempt

Yes that man got plenty
              — too much perhaps
    if you can judge
from the washed out expression
              he's been wearing lately

TRADITION

Eat with your right hand
Wipe your ass with your left
And if it happens
    that you're left-handed
Man, you're in trouble

STANCE

Both Christ and Buddha knew
Even the most defensive action
Can turn aggressive. Witness
That big-boobed librarian who remains
Peering at something on her desk
I suddenly say "Ahhem!" and she
Straightens up, pointing them at me
Like two ICBM's with nuclear tips

TRANSPORT

When Charley was old enough
to get his driver's licence
he bought an old Chevy sedan
and set up Betty his girl friend
in the back seat
for three dollars a crack
among his school chums
and after a while
he started to get a few
outside customers as well
and this gave him the idea
of trading the jalopy in
on a used hearse, a move
which just happened to co-incide
with a new morality campaign
brought in by the City Council
the effect of which closed down
most of the existing cat houses
for some months and WOW
business boomed for Charley
to such an extent that soon
he'd got enough financial backing
to establish a city-wide fleet
of "lay-on-the-way" cars, or
to use the vulgar term
"whore-hearses", each of them

a big shiny black Caddy
with uniformed driver and
foam mattress and miniature bar
and Charley had all the cars
equipped with two-way radios
so the central office
could dispatch them to your door
within minutes of a call

At first all the action
took place at night
but after Charley switched
to another Public Relations firm
the thing really began to catch on
with business men
ordering Charley's cars
to get to luncheon appointments
or executive conferences
so they could screw away their tensions
without feeling guilty
about loosing time
Eventually Charley cashed in
on the commuter market
in all the major cities
and after introducing special rates
for short inter-urban hops
he ended with a vast network
of mobile bordellos
speeding from coast to coast
across the nation

As you probably recall
Charley's letterhead
used to bear a flying ram
encircled by the motto
Come as You Go
and Arrive Satisfied

Yes Charley played it smart
and made a pile while it lasted
because in those days
no one had thought
of legislating against, for example
"keeping a disorderly automobile"
though once Charley
got into a scrape
for having red lights
on top of his vehicles
instead of at the rear

But strangely enough
Charley's real trouble came
from the "PROFESSIONAL BROTHERHOOD
OF SMILING MORTICIANS"
who were being increasingly
plagued by people who would
flag down funeral processions
and try to climb in with the stiff

As could be expected
with that kind of opposition
the enactment of stringent
anti-sex road laws
finally put an end to the era
of the travelling orgasm
but by that time Charley
had already sold out and invested
in the munitions industry where
profits were ten times
as high, and the future
unequivocally secure

After that Charley
found himself rich enough
to slip easily into
high level politics
(I suppose it was still
the spirit of public service
which prompted him) and today
few people remember
the imagination and drive
that characterized his youth

Though I've got a hunch it was
as a kind of tribute
to Charley's remarkable background
that the Prime Minister first
made him Minister of Transport
before switching him to Defence

And incidentally I've heard it said
that even today Old Charley
shows a passing interest
in the social, as well as
the military potential
of helicopters and hovercraft

ELECTROPOET

Roger used to be content sticking electrodes into his scalp in order to record his dreams directly on video tape which he played back later over closed circuit TV. But now that he's grown ambitious Roger talks of broadcasting them live and in color and attaining total coverage and instantaneous response by plugging in his imagination to the national microwave network. It is doubtful however if the Board of Broadcast Governors will grant Roger a licence at this early stage in the development of his medium so he'll probably be forced to put his head into orbit and beam his images at us from beyond the twelve mile limit.

INFLATION

"Good-bye, Skin," I said, shaking his hand and noticing how creased and wrinkled he'd become

"Now I know we've been pretty close during the last year," I went on, trying to cheer him up a little, "but even so there's no point in looking down and out"

And suddenly, thinking of an appropriate farewell gesture, I grabbed him quick and sealed up all his openings with rubber cement

That is, with the exception of his left nostril which I made into a kind of valve

Then, turning him completely inside out, I inflated him with hydrogen

The change in his aspect was remarkable, even more dramatic than that brought about by a Mable Slick-Chick Nova Epidermus Beauty treatment

Yes you should have seen the expression of bliss on his face as he left the ground

As a matter of fact it was probably the best high he'd ever had

And as I watched him disappear from view I thought of the bang he was going to get out of it when he lit his pipe

SUBVERSION

I can't stand smoking
    Vowed the reclining nude
A smouldering cigarette
    Protruding from her vulva
And a thin line of fumes
    Coiling around her leg

FORM

"In struggling against
the limitations imposed
by the form, the poet
creates poetic tension"

That's why Harold always
inscribes his poems
on the point of a needle

The scholars of course
like nothing better
than putting Harold's poems
under the microscope

And I'll admit lately
I've been digging
some of them myself
as you probably see
by the scars on my arm

PATRIOTIC POEM

Oh Canada, you two-bit whore
You ARE knocked up! And who
Would have thought you had it
In you? The word is that a mysterious
Dark gentleman tried to beguile you
With exuberant promises and sweet
Prophecy. You had him thrown out
Of course, being bent on maintaining
A respectable clientele, but he
Returned later that night, climbed in
Quietly through a window, and before
You could re-insert your diaphragm
He'd given it to you good, at least
That's what they say, and it's evident
That something happened. Yes you're
In bad shape, Old Girl. In fact it looks
Like you're coming apart at the seams.
I guess those abortion attempts hurt you
more than the kid. Good God

Look at him kicking and punching!
I can see the action right through
Your dress. Makes those maple leaves
In the pattern seem like they're
Blowing in the wind. You say you
Hate the brat already? Well I
Don't imagine he'll waste much love
On you either, Old Mum. Probably
Won't even talk English to you
If I know anything. But don't worry
Yourself too much about that part
Of it, because I doubt if you'll even
Survive the birth. O Canada
There always was something fishy
About you, and right now you remind me
Of a coho salmon: spawning, you'll die
Leaving your torn and battered carcass
To rot on the river bank, a meal
For the scavenging eagle or bear

RELIGIOUS POEM

On Sundays
Alphonse usually
switched to
Benedictine

Considering his
Catholic background
it was the
least he could do

CHRISTMAS POEM

Santa Claus, having considered
your distribution policy in detail
we have at last discovered
your *true* political colour.
We should have guessed it
when you grew so fat
but your peasant face
and your ho-ho-ho had us fooled.
Oh you're a smoothie alright, Santa,
playing the Give-Away-King
while everyone's asleep. Of course
you appear on appropriate occasions,
dandle kiddies on your knee,
subscribe to worthy charities,
but when it comes right down to it
you're just out to enforce
the status-quo. The truth is
that you leave great bundles of toys
at the homes of rich children
and practically nothing in the slums.
So hear this, Santa, we will not
participate in your Christmas Party
and as far as we're concerned
you can take your red suit
and cram it, because we prefer green.
It's Robin Hood's colour

KINETIC POEM

"The poem is a machine" said that famous man and so I'm
  building one
Or at least I'm having it built, because I want something big
  and impressive and automatic
You see, people will stand in front of it and insert money,
  dimes or quarters depending on the poem's locus
Yes the whole thing will clank and hum and light up and issue
  a string of words on colored ticker-tape
Or maybe the customers will wear ear-phones and turn small
  knobs so the experience will be more audile-tactile than
  old fashioned visual
In any case they'll only get one line at a time
This being the most important feature of my design which is
  based on the principle that
In poetry "One perception must immediately and directly lead
  to a further perception"
And therefore the audience will be compelled to feed in coin
  after coin

Now I admit that this prototype model that you see on display
  is something of a compromise as it has a live poet
  concealed inside
But I assure you this crudity will eventually be eliminated
Because each machine is to be fully computerized
And so able to stand on its own two feet

PARTICIPATORY POEM

It has begun. Already the poets are working their cybernetic voodoo
Soon the thousand-foot television screens that have been set up in front of every house
Will light up automatically and display lifesize images of themselves
And God will be manifest as an enormous eye looking everywhere and in both directions
That is, from the inside out, and from the outside in, simultaneously
It is difficult to speculate as to the developments after this stage
But some of the more imaginative among us believe that

The reader is asked to complete the poem himself in the space remaining on the page

61

VENTILATION

Peter Paranoid tokes his grass
        while sitting on his pot
     the only place in the world
      where he feels safe
toke toke toke . . . one hand poised ready
        to fling exhibit A
    into the toilet bowl
        and flush it quick
     at the least sound
    or sign of disturbance
He has the bathroom door locked
  and the vent-fan turned on full
    to evacuate the tell-tale scent
for Peter Paranoid takes no chances
        or so he believes
      being unaware
    that at this very moment
Detective Slippery Sam Snuff
  at the head of his ten-man nark squad
      is being led
   by Rosebud the Roach-Headed Retriever
    down through
the labyrinthine connections
  of the building's ventilation system

What will transpire?
Peter is stepping off the bathroom scales
        having checked his weight
against his rapidly increasing height
    and saying to his grass-headed image
            in the mirror
that in actuality the lavatory
    is a reasonably designed toking room
            though perhaps a bit cramped
        for a large gathering of heads
and just as Peter is considering the
            the feasibility
        of extending the far wall
    and installing half a dozen more pots
the vent-fan suddenly cuts out
        and the long thin hand
    of Detective Slippery Sam Snuff
reaches stealthily through the louvres
        to grasp Peter by the throat
"Not another toke, you criminal" says Sam
    while Rosebud leaps down
            to catch the roach in mid air
        as Peter tries to throw it
            into the toilet

During the brief struggle that ensues
      Detective Slippery calls for his squad
            to climb down and do their duty
and is surprised at their lack of response
      for it seems that the thought
            of making a violent arrest

in the seclusion of a private bathroom
      has given all the men
            massive erections
            lodging them firmly
in the ventilation pipe

Nevertheless Detective Slippery Sam Snuff
      acting in the manner recommended
            in his pocket manual
      of basic police strategy
is kicking Peter Paranoid in the chest
      and trying to trap
            the expelled illegal air
in a special polyethaline bag
      designed specifically for that purpose
            for it seems that Rosebud
has swallowed all the other
            tangible evidence

"Confound that greedy roach-head"
　　　snorts Detective Slippery
"Next thing we know that mut
will be dropping acid
　　　on police department time"
and at that moment
　　　as Slippery
switches on the ceiling sun-lamp
　　　in an attempt to simulate
　　a more orthodox interrogation scene
Peter jumps into the toilet bowl
　　　and flushes himself down
　　along with Rosebud
　　　his new found best friend
leaving the astounded detective
　　　alone in the john
　　getting a sun-tan
　　　and holding a bag
of Peter Paranoid's bad breath
and although you may not believe it
　　perhaps for the first time
　　　in his career
　　Slippery Sam Snuff
　　　has begun to smile
　　for the fumes in the room
are having their effect
　　and even the men in pipe
　　　are asking Sam
　　to turn on the vent fan
so they too can enjoy
　　　a bit of a lift

Today Peter Paranoid
          does all his toking
     in the septic tank
thinking it's the safest place possible
     because the smoke
          can't get by
     the vapour-locks in the drains
though there are other dangers down there
     like the time Peter
tried to walk on the water
               and almost drown
          before Rosebud could retrieve him

And as for Detective Slippery Sam Snuff
     he recovered his usual
                    policeman personality
     on reaching the fresh air
and since that terrible experience
     he now makes it a rule
          to wear a gas-mask
     in any similar situation

However
it is difficult to say exactly
what has become
of those brave members of the nark squad
who were caught in the pipe
for although the police department
denies the rumour
that they are still somewhere
in the ventilating system
the tenants in the building
are troubled
by a pervading bad smell
and some of them
have a strange feeling
that they are being watched
even in the privacy of their bathrooms

ECONOMIC CHRONOLOGY

I was standing there
growing my beard
and finger nails
while my car
resting in the garage
depreciated
       at approximately
fifty cents an hour

COLOR PROBLEM

Her hair was black
Her skin was white
But when the truth
     was made evident
She had a green pudendum

ART

I'm always writing
except when I'm
committing suicide
or making love

ROLES

The difference is that when inspiration hits me I make it into a
   poem
Like today when I'm thinking why not a beauty cream that
   not only looks good and smells good *but tastes good too*
Wow can you imagine the appetizing dishes that could be
   prepared mmmmmmmmmmmmmmmm ... and all the
   delicious advertising copy
At last a chance to integrate the senses and appreciate woman
   in depth
Anyway I want you to make special note of it so that in times
   to come you may bear witness to the truth
That it was me, Lionel Kearns, poet, who first thought of it on
   July 26, 1968, while I was walking down the street on the
   way to the fish store
Because undoubtedly someone else will steal the idea, patent
   it, and make himself a pile
In fact that's what I mean —
That's the difference

THE SEVENTH SEAL

This is the story of the Seventh Seal
                who wasn't really a seal at all
but an imaginative young Polar Bear
                who wanted to become one
        You see
there was this small community
                of impoverished Eskimos
who for years had been preyed upon
        by a pack
        of stealthy
and seemingly invincible
                Wolves

        The Eskimos worked hard all year
carving little figurines in stone
        and printing out a few Christmas cards
but every year
        just as they were getting ready
                for their Thanksgiving Festival
and looking forward to their slack season
        when they would be able to sit back
and rest and dance and make love
                in the intimacy of their kyaks
or under the comfort of their warm blankets
                it would happen

BAM! BAM! BAM!
the Wolves would be roaring in
on their sporty new Ski-Doo snow scooters
and their big powerful Bombardier snow-mobiles
to gather up the whole year's produce
while the Eskimos
standing around shivering with fright
would anticipate another winter
without adequate clothing or food or oil
to burn in their lamps
to brighten the midday gloom of their igloos

For a few days the Wolves would stalk around town
shooting up the restaurants
and ravishing Eskimo girls in the snowbanks
whenever they could get their paws on them
It was also the Wolves' policy
to force the whole population to eat shit

"Damn good for ya, Boy"
they would say
"Nothing like a mouth full of Wolf-turd
to make an Eskimo realize what's what"

Although this kind of behavior
                may seem like mere perversity
           it was in fact
an important and integral part
           of the Wolves' overall program
for according to the economic ideology
                to which they subscribed
           trade must follow conquest

Were they to take in the wealth
           of the Eskimo villagers
     without forcing something of their own
           on their victims
     the whole Wolf economy would collapse
           because of the inflationary pressure
brought on by an unfavorable balance of payments
     and so it was that the Wolves
           exported great quantities of shit
                creating a demand for it
           by T.V. advertising
           phoney sweep-stakes
                and free gift coupons

This was the pattern year after year
with the Eskimos becoming more and more broken
in spirit and health
a few even felt lucky
to be left alive at all
and these were the ones
who would go out and welcome the Wolves
and fawn on them
hoping to win some small favour
such as the exclusive right to distribute
a new flavour of Wolf-shit
or the local franchise
to collect the empty cartons

But there were others among the Eskimos
who had different ideas
"Better to die than eat shit"
they whispered to one another
"Let's fight"

The Eskimos however
had no knowledge or experience of conflict
and for this reason they determined
to enlist the support of some Seals
who in those days
were traditionally bred and trained
in the skills of maintaining human dignity

"Do you think the proud Seals
will humble themselves
by defending us
poor Eskimos that we are?"
"I think so
as long as we do not degrade ourselves
by eating shit in their presence"

And so the Eskimos sent off a secret delegation
to try to persuade the Seals to help them
and as it turned out
they were able to find six willing Seals
and one Polar Bear
who wanted to become one

At first the other Seals resented the presence
of this outsider in their ranks
because of his unorthodox proposals
such as shooting flowers at the Wolves
instead of bullets
however the Seals eventually
grew to love and respect him
for ultimately it was this Polar Bear
who was to play
the most significant role in the struggle
as you will learn in a moment

To begin with the Seals organized the Eskimos
and taught them how to defend themselves
and how to see through the semantic traps
of the Wolf-Shit advertisements
but when the Wolves discovered what was going on
they zoomed in with napalm and poison gas
and lazy-dog fragmenting anti-personnel bombs
which killed a large number of Eskimos
especially women and children

Immediately the Eskimo Resistance struck back
installing booby traps along the ski-trails
ambushing lonely Wolf-patrols
mining snow fields and frozen rivers
or attacking isolated Wolf-holes

Each day the conflict grew more intense and bitter
      because from the Wolves' point of view
            exporting death
         was as economically advantageous
               as exporting shit
and as far as the Eskimos were concerned
      fighting to the death
               was better than eating it

So the struggle went on and on
            with no real solution in sight
      until the Seventh Seal
            being a Polar Bear
      made his way through the enemy lines
   to do some reconnoitering back in Wolfland
where he found to his great surprise
         that some of the Wolves
               especially the younger ones
weren't actually as inhuman as he had once believed

      Their problem
         as he saw it
      stemmed from the fact
   that they were all hooked on their own product
         the shit they were consuming
      was poisoning their souls
break their habit
      he thought
   and he would abolish
            the monstrous spectre of Wolfhood

And so while the massive Wolf armies
          with all their technological superiority
               were battering the Eskimo village
     and trying to contend
          with the roving bands
                    of Seal-led Eskimo guerrillas
     who would tunnel through the snow
               to attack the Wolves in the flank
     the Seventh Seal
               who was really a Polar Bear
was hoofing it around Wolfland
          showing the Wolf-kids
                    how to turn on with poetry

          "You just take a poem
               roll it into a joint
                    and smoke it"
          and they did
                    and they liked it
     and they told their friends
and before long a whole generation of young Wolves
               was turning away
          from the excremental habits of their parents
               for as everyone knows
Poetry is the most efficient means
          of counteracting a taste for shit

          "Come on now Mum"
               the kids would say
          "Stop eating that stuff for a minute
                    and sit down here with me
     and we'll have a quiet toke on this here poem OK?"
               it was
               REVOLUTION

Increasingly the practice developed
               even among the older Wolves
of burying their shit instead of eating it
               and with this radical change of diet
they stopped growling and snarling at one another
       and to their own amazement
               they became interested in things like
       love and creation
and some of them started carving in stone themselves
       and printing out Christmas cards
               of their own

               Gradually the Wolves realized
there was no need for the war at all
               and so they gave it up
of course the Eskimos welcomed the truce
       and returned to their former
               simple and productive lives

And so it came to pass
               that with peace and food and poems
       distributed over the land
       and all the shit safely under it
the Wolves and the Seals and the Polar Bear
               who was the Seventh Seal
       and the Eskimos all
settled down to love one another and rejoice
       in the warmth and dignity
               of their own humanity